Amatel

Amanda Whittington

SERVING THEATRE

S F

SINCE 1830

SAMUELFRENCH-LONDON.CO.UK

SAMUELFRENCH.COM

FOR AMATEUR PRODUCTION ENQUIRIES

UNITED KINGDOM AND WORLD EXCLUDING NORTH AMERICA
plays@SamuelFrench-London.co.uk
020 7255 4302/01

UNITED STATES AND CANADA
info@SamuelFrench.com
1-866-598-8449

Each title is subject to availability from Samuel French, depending upon country of performance.

PRODUCTION HISTORY

Amateur Girl was originally written as a 15-minute episode of the
BBC Radio 4 Woman's Hour drama, *Minimum Wages 2*. It was broadcast on
January 30, 2007, and produced by Paul Dodgson with the
following cast:

JULIE – Katharine Rogers

The stage play of *Amateur Girl* was commissioned and produced by Hull Truck
Theatre, opening on June 11th 2009. It was directed by Nick Lane with the
following cast:

JULIE – Julie Riley

The play was subsequently co-produced by Fifth Word Theatre and Nottingham
Playhouse, opening on February 3rd, 2014, prior to a national tour. It was directed
by Kate Chapman with the following cast:

JULIE – Lucy Speed

JULIE is an auxiliary nurse from Nottingham.

Scene One

January. **JULIE**'s *flat, Victoria Centre, Nottingham.* **JULIE** *comes in from work. She takes off her coat.*

JULIE. *(calls)* Lulu?

JULIE *puts a few cat biscuits into a dish.*

Twelve hour shifts...dunno why I bother coming home. Well, I do. *(calls)* Lulu? She's 10 now but she were three when I got her. Rescue cat. Right scumbags from St Ann's had her first. Kicked her so hard she went deaf. I call her name, all the same. She might hear the vibrations. You're not allowed pets in the flat but I say "Stuff 'em". Not the cats, the council. She's no trouble. She don't care she's twelve flights up, she don't want to go out. Sleeps most of the day. Nice life, I could do wi' a bit. Nights like this, you might as well live on that ward.

JULIE *pours a glass of white wine.*

Still, she's good to me, Matron. Sorry, Ward Manager. She's lovely and loves me to bits. Has me over for barbecues, all sorts. I work hard for her too, you have to wi' elderly. There's nowt wrong with most of 'em, they're lonely, that's all or they've given up. I have a laugh and a joke with 'em: cheeky daft, me. I call the docs by their first names: "You've gorra nice bum". I'm not disrespectful, it's just how I am. I was in the *Evening Post* for it. A man on his death bed got well and wrote in. He said: "Thank you to Julie, who's mad and crazy and kept us all laughing." Have to, don't yer? Sometimes, you go ten days through wi'out a break. Come home at midnight, nod off on the sofa, back in for seven.

Lulu?

Mornings are the worst. There's no time for chatting, you're straight on the ward. Auxiliaries do personal care and hygiene. If patients are in urine or they've messed themselves or been sick in the night then you strip 'em, take the bedding and wash

1

'em top to toe. You have to scrub between their legs cos they get little cysts when they're wet. You make sure they're properly dry – no creams though or talc. Change the sheets, make the bed, sit them up and feed 'em. If they can't swallow, it's a PEG feed; that's a plastic lead through their belly, the doc puts that in. You make sure they get fluids, wet their lips with a sponge, if you don't they go dry and get blisters. And pressure sores, I do them, an' all. Change the dressings and chat. Talk of the past, what they've done in their life. They'll ask, "Are you married?" "Not me, duck. Y'offering?" I don't bring up my boyfriend. Well, I say boyfriend, he's just a bloke I know. Casual, like, I don't do hearts and flowers. I'd rather have fun with the girls. Blimey, what we get up to, we'd all get the boot if they knew. *(calls)* Lu?

One thing we're mad on is Take That. We've got all the CDs, we play 'em on't ward. Beautiful World, an' that. Progress. A while back, we hear they're on tour. Not just the four of them – five. We've not got the cash but we're dying – we're dying – to go. Matron knows how hard we've been working, says: "Leave it to me". She gets on the phone to, well, I dunno, someone, the manager:

"Thing is, you see, we've got two poorly girls on the ward. They haven't got long and their very last wish is to see 'em together again cos they're such massive fans."

Weren't a lie, not as such, we were fans. We are.

There's an old ambulance, it runs patients all round the site. Matron pulls a few strings, gets the keys, off we go. Me and Shaz as the girls and our 'carers'. A milk float goes faster but somehow it gets us to Villa Park. Two great big bouncers come out. I think, 'that's it, we're done for' but Matron, she flashes her badge and we're in. We look the part, we've got drips in, no make-up, we're both sat in wheelchairs but still... I thought I were dreaming... front row.

Sounds of the concert flood the flat.

Lights go down. Girls are screaming and shouting and there they are: Mark, Jason, Howard and Gary. In the flesh, right there and real. "Rule the World", "Patience". Robbie comes on, does his stuff, then the others come back. "One for each of us", Shaz says. And I know – I know – that right at that moment, he looked at me, straight in the eye. And summat inside me goes "Gary!" out loud. I jump up out my wheelchair, Matron says "Oi, you're disabled" but come on, you have to, it's once-in-a-lifetime, in't it?

We danced all night after that, we didn't care. And we don't mean no harm. It's a bit of fun, that's all. Summat to do, to remember. And like the song says, I'll never forget it. Not till my last dying day.

The concert dissolves away.

Next morning at work, the girls are reliving it all. I'm laughing but I dunno, inside I'm not. For the first time in years, I go sick. Go to bed, staring at Gary, up there on the wall. Thinking, but not. You get up in the end, what else can you do? Put on a smile, go to work. Go out. And that's when I met him. Not Gary Barlow, I wish. But he's chunky, like him. Same name, same cheeky smile. It's a funny coincidence, ey?

See, we go the Palais too, me and the girls. Well, the Palais, as was. There's a lad we know, Mickey – male stripper. Good body. Good laugh. Good shag. And he's got this mate, Gary. Introduced us last month. "This is Julie, she's mad", and I bloody was that night, I tell yer. It's Christmas. I've gone out as a tree. Wrapped up in tinsel with a fairy on my head and great big silver baubles for earrings. I go down in the lift and past Denzil from Security. "You'll catch your death", he says. Nice lad, looks out for me. Anyway, Gary. He's 42, so he says. Pierced ear, gelled hair. I like him straight off but I weren't letting on. "You need your roots done, you", I says "What do you mean? I'm dirty blonde. Bet you're into that, ey?" Turns out he's married but at least he's up front. "I won't lie to you, Julie. I love my wife but I can't be a one-woman man".

JULIE *takes off her work shoes and puts on a pair of heels.*

Fine by me. Last thing I want is an 'usband. Been there, done that. Well, I weren't technically married, though it felt like I was. Don't get me wrong, he weren't a bad bloke. Too good to last, I suppose. Col were 30, I'm 18, met in the pub as you do. And it felt great at first; leaving home; moving in; cooking tea when he came off his shift. He's bought his own house, done it up: new bathroom, conservatory. Thing is, he's more like a mate, I suppose. He never bothers me much for s.e.x. He'd

rather watch telly. Wildlife programmes. 'Insects in the Congo'
or wherever they were. On my twenty-first birthday, he gives me
a ring. I think 'Julie, you're sorted. Nice house, nice husband, a
couple of kids to come. Yep, this is the rest of your life.' So what
do I do? Get me moods. Give up work. Sit round all day in me
dressing gown. The more he says he understands, the worse I
get. Dunno why. But I do know he'd be better without me. One
afternoon, I just pack me bags, get on a bus. End up here, cut
a long story short. Vicky Centre, bang in the middle of town.
Freedom. Independence. If I want a bloke, yeh, I'll have one. If
I don't, then I don't—

The buzzer sounds.

And tonight, as it happens, I do.

Scene Two

March. Post-midnight. **JULIE** *is wearing a basque. She moves to the mirror, viewing herself from every angle. As she turns, she is caught in a rapid-fire camera flash.*

JULIE. I got a red reminder today. Winter quarter, the worst: three hundred-and-twenty-six quid. I leave it on low when I'm out, see, for Lulu. Electric's gone up to forty a month, Council Tax is a hundred-and-twenty and that's with the discount. I spent seventeen quid in Tesco last night just on cat food. And vodka. We take it out in our handbag, you have to. "You're down there too much, you", says Matron. "Why can't you stop in with a film?" "You're joking, aren't you? Where's the fun in that, ey?" And that's all it is, this – a bit of fun. Yeh. And a few extra quid for the bills.

It were a month to the day since we met. Not that I'm counting. I'm just in from work when he phones. "Julie, I've got summat to share with you." I thought it must be a pizza but up he comes with a camera. Right professional, great big long lens. "Best way to look at a beautiful girl." "Girl?" "Say cheese." Turns out photography's one of his hobbies. Goes to a club. He's got me doing all sorts, in my uniform, then not. I says "You'd better not be showing these around." "We're consenting adults, Julie. What's the problem? And we're having a good time, aren't we?"

A camera flashes.

I feel funny at first but he's ever so good. Gives you all sorts of praise, puts you at ease. "You've never modelled? You sure? You're a natural, you know?" The more he goes on, the more I… go on. A bit further than I should have I suppose but like he says, we're grown-ups. We have a drink and a laugh and a bit of the other then he whips out this men's magazine. Girls on sofas like mine. Looks like a dirty DFS ad. Well, I say girls, not all of 'em are. "Over-40-Still-Naughty", says Gary. "A hundred quid for a picture. Shall we send one or what?" I had

5

to laugh. "Of me? Who'd want to wotsit to me? It's lasses with implants they're after." Gary turns and looks me straight in the eye. "Julie, you've got Premiership looks but you're talking like you're third division." And he meant it. He did. "I'd be dead proud to see you in print".

Flash-flash-flash.

And nowadays, of course, you don't have to take 'em to Boots. You can upload 'em all on his laptop. I get to look at 'em – one click, the bad uns are gone. "What if your wife see all this?" "Open marriage", he says. There's a club for that, too. "So, shall we go for it, Julie? I don't want the cash. If they're printed, it's yours".

Flash-flash-flash.

Funny what goes through your head when he's gone. All sorts of daft things. Like where are the photos of me as a kid? I know they were took, Mam kept 'em in a shoebox under the stairs. There was one in the backyard, me a babe in her arms. Fair scowling at the camera, she was. One outside a caravan, Butlins behind us. We stayed on the site across the road, saw it all through the wire. One sat by a Christmas tree, tinsel. One in an old toy car. One with me dad before he died. One when she married me stepdad. Age twelve and face like thunder. One where I'm five years old in the snow: blue anorak, woolly hat, mittens. Smile like the sun. I wonder what happened to that?

I went to work and thought no more about it. A hundred quid? Right! They'll want snaps of young 'uns, not me, no way. Goes clear out my mind with a bug on the ward. All three auxiliaries off sick and I'm the mug what don't catch it. Twelve-hour shifts for a week and a half. Wednesday, I come out of work and he's sat there, parked up in his car. Tinted windows. Heated seats. "Good news, Julie. You're a winner." "I'm a what?" "Your pic's won a prize." "A hundred quid prize?" "And the rest. They want to meet us, tomorrow." "But Gary, I'm working, they need me, we're—"

"Bloody hell, Ju. Say you've got the lurgy an' all." And I have, in a way, I'm all churned up inside. A winner, me? I go to work, go out, have a laugh and that's it. I don't get whisked off in flash cars by good-looking blokes. I don't get chauffeured to London. Not me.

Gary laughed when I said I'd not been there before. "London virgin? So where shall I take you? Nelson's Column, you know that? Big Ben?" I couldn't think of owt but that old gal who feeds the birds, tuppence a bag. I watched it with Dad every Christmas, I started to tell him but: "That's a film, Julie, for kids. Friggin' hell".

He went a bit quiet after that. S'alright. I liked it just being with him. Properly with him, walking around, on a real date, with dinner. Gourmet Burger Kitchen. Food on a posh piece of wood. "Well, you're worth it, aren't yer? Drink up".

Sounds of London streets flood the flat.

Gary pays. Leaves a tip. "We'll walk it to Soho." 'In these shoes', I think. But it's dark now and oh, it's like Goose Fair but better. The lights, the taxis, the West End theatres. "Look, The Bodyguard's on, can we go?" But Gary just says "Can't you walk any quicker?" Didn't mean it. I've never been to a theatre, I wouldn't know how. Me mam and stepdad didn't do things like that. I dunno what they did, looking back. Stay in, watch telly, play horrible records. Johnny Cash and Jim Reeves. Every Sunday morning, he'd sing along to 'Old Shep'. Making out like he's moved. I'd go under the covers. Blot it all out. His whistling, his coughing, his tread on the stairs... I'd lie there going "You're here but you're not, Ju. You're here but you're not".

We go up a street with a market on, fruit and veg, then down an alley. Smells of cabbage. Back door and creaky old stairs, six flights up to a studio. That's what he says it is, anyway. Big lights and a bloke with a lens even longer than Gary's. Shakes Gary's hand: "Nice to see you again." Says he's called Rocky. Nods to the camera. "What do you think of your prize, then?" "I've won that?" "You've won a top-class shoot here with Tina. The blonde doing her hair." I said "Hang on a minute, I've not brought my stuff." "Not to worry. Go shopping, I'll talk to your manager." Manager? Gary gives us a look that says "don't say a word." Rocky pulls out his wallet. Takes out the hundred quid. "Tina? Get Jackie sorted with this."

Sound of the quick-firing camera shutter.

Julie.

But still, she were lovely, Tina. Dead pally. Buys us this basque. Gets us waxed. Takes us to a wine bar, it's eight quid a glass. She goes "It's his money, let's have a bottle." It's mine though, I won it. I don't say that though. She says not to worry, she's done it before, there's nowt to it. "Girls night out, best mates, we're drunk and we're having a laugh." "Well, I can do that. You should see me out with the girls." Not that I go kissing 'em, mind. I've nowt against it; it's just not my thing. Still, like Tina says, it's for the camera, that's all. And once we've done it, I don't really mind. She feels strange… soft all over… but nice, in a funny way. Nice.

By the end of it all, it's gone midnight. Rocky's grinning and Gary, he's over the moon. "Sod this, I'm not driving home." We go out for drinks. Spend the whole night together in Rocky's spare room. Properly together. "I've not met no-one like you, Julie. You'll go anywhere, do owt. You don't know the meaning of no". It's what we were smoking I suppose but I've never… not with any man… I've never felt special before.

Gary can just about drive with his hangover. Drops me at home. "Coming in?" "Not now, luv. People to see, an' all that." I feel a bit stupid. He takes out his wallet. "Fifty quid, Ju. For expenses. Good work." I have a shower, get changed, go out. I'm dog-rough when I get to the ward. "You shouldn't be here", Matron says. "But I want to, I'm better", I say. And I want to tell her, I want to say: "This one, he's different. He's not like Col and he's nowt like Aaron." The twat I lived with before. He got sent down in the end, threw a lad through a window at Southern Fried Chicken. "No, this one's… he's a businessman. He's got plans. Proper plans." But say that and I'll have to say what. Then she'll know that I'm planning to go.

Sound of the camera shutter.

What's that film called… not Frankenstein… Jekyll and Hyde! Half of me's is stripping beds, feeding folk, cleaning their mess. The other half's up on the top shelf. I'm not a cover girl – 'Not yet' – but I'm featured. Full colour, full… you know. The first time he brings 'em, you feel… I dunno… I can't say for sure. It's you staring back but it's not… In one magazine, your name's Kimberly, in another, you're Alex, another, you're Sam. Gary says it's part of the fun, changing your name. Part of the fantasy.

Sound of the camera shutter.

I think 'God, if somebody sees 'em at work. If Matron...' But like Gary says, what I do in my own time's my business. "They don't own you, not on them wages. With this, you'll make more in a day than you do in a week. More in a week than a month. Well, if that's what you want?"

The camera flashes.

Turns out Gary's got a camcorder. Top-of-the-range. Says it's dead easy these days, with technology. You make the films cheap and sell 'em online. "And every girl starts with a showreel." Not me! "Why not? Just for the hell of it, just for a laugh?"

The camera flashes.

I was in a play once. *Aladdin.* I were Girl In Laundry and I loved it. Loved it. When I was sixteen, I asked to do drama at college. Me step-dad stubs out his fag. "Drama? What good'll that do yer? Who do know who's famous from Mansfield?" I tell Gary. He says I'm worth more than that. More than the minimum wage. "We'll go 50/50 on all of it, Julie. Trust me. You'll be made."

Tonight at work, an old gal passed away. She was eighty. Dementia. No family, no nothing. I laid her out, did me best. Still... it makes you look back on the things you've done. Things you've not done. Makes you think... makes you think you should live for today. Makes you text him: 'Bring camera 2night'.

Shit.

But like Gary says, it's not about glamour no more. Men want girls in their own home, them who look like your neighbour, your best mate's wife, them who you could have in real life.

Amateur girls.

Sound of the buzzer pierces the silence.

And he's right. Why not? Just for the hell of it. Just for a laugh.

Scene Three

June. 9pm. **JULIE** *puts on make-up and vigorously sprays her hair.*

JULIE. I went right through the flat before they came. Dusted, polished, pulled out the sofa, hoovered the back. Well, you don't know where they'll want yer. Cleaned the bathroom, there's dye up the tiles, I get it all over, can't help it. When they've paid me, I thought, I'm having highlights in a salon, proper ones, with foil. I'll get a St. Tropez an' all, no more fake-tan streaky-bacon stuff. Cos like Gary says, we'll be minted.

They liked my showreel. This crew Gary knows *(that's short for production crew)* wanted to work with us ASAP. Two weeks later, they're on their way up. Denzil, Security, buzzes me: "What's going on?" "Mind your own, you perv." I hang up and next minute, he knocks on. "It's my job to keep watch on all this." "Yeh, from a distance. Piss off." He knows I don't mean it. Good lad, is Denzil. He gave Aaron a pasting, he never came back. You need that if you live on your own. Bit of muscle behind you. Bit of a drink and a laugh on a quiet night in. "Turn a blind eye. Come up Sunday", I says. "We'll watch a film, shall we", he winks. He's sent 'em all up in the lift, see? Two cameramen, sound man, lighting man; young lass called Natalie, Natalie's manager; Gary, Gary's wife. She does make-up. Nice girl. Friendlyish. Big lips and Botox, stick thin. She keeps fit Salsa dancing, goes five nights a week. "Gary does his thing and I do mine. It's like Sting says: if you love somebody, set them free".

Lulu don't like her. I shut her away in the bedroom, they set up the gear. Takes bloody ages. But while I'm making the tea, I get talking to one of the cameraman and I couldn't believe it: he's only David Beckham's brother. You can see it as soon as he says. Same tattoos. He does acting an' all but he wears a hood. Can't be identified, obviously. Natalie knows him, she says he's always a gentleman. Scarborough, she's from. Smells of cider. Been at it a year. She wants to be famous and rich, not for her, for her little boy. Wants him to have a good life. Good education. Ambitious, see? Like me.

So eventually, midday, we start. Turns out there's no story as such. No lines like in Corrie or owt, we just make 'em up.

Improvise. Big relief. Words on a page, it's not me. School went over my head. I'd go into myself and off on one. Make up all sorts of things…or just sit there and… nothing at all. Silence. Black as the board.

Sorry.

So they film us in the flat, then going down in the lift, then to the car park. First surprise: great big convertible, hired out for the day. Natalie drives. Beckham's brother in the back and a 4-by-4 filming behind. We go right through town: London Road, up Maid Marion Way. People are staring, lads pap their horns. We have to say things like "It's hot in here", take off our clothes. We follow Gary. A60, A614. Sherwood Forest. Out of the car and more hanging round while they set up the shots. They give us these little white skirts to wear. White socks. Gary's wife does our hair up in plaits. We have to look like girls doing PE, which is a laugh in itself cos I were the last to be picked, every time. I'd stand with the fat lass and the one wi' a twitch and think "What have I done? It's not my fault I live in the scruffiest house and… and my stepdad's a… and Mam never says nothing at all."

But anyway, finally… it's a nice spring day. There's people around, you know, walking the dog, little kids holding hands with their mams. Folk stare as we're filming. Gary says "Walk", so we do. We walk for-bloody-ever, to a field in the middle of nowhere. Lads are there playing football. Six-a-side, jumpers for goalposts, all that. "Keep walking", says Gary. But then the lads, they start shouting, calling us names, bad names, dead rough and nasty. One goes "Look at them slags." I shout back cos that's me, I stand up to bullies, I learned that from school days, I tell yer. But then they come after us. Chasing us. "Leggit", says Gary and so we do. Cameras, everything. Into the woods.

Sound of heavy breathing as a woman runs through the woods.

We're running and running but they're getting closer. I nearly trip over and fall. And when they finally catch us, the cameras kept filming. Turns out they're part of it, part of the film. It's set up like they're raping us, see? And it's our job to serve 'em. All twelve of 'em.

Sound of breathing stops abruptly.

(Babes in the Wood) Gary said it looked dead realistic. Gave us two hundred pounds, cash-in-hand. Said it's just the beginning. If I stick with him, I could have me own house just like his, in Arnold. Brand new, five bedrooms, three loos and a woman to come in and clean 'em. We ended up there after filming. Red wine and charlie. I said: "Gary, stop, I'm at work in the morning". "That's Julie talking". "Who else?" "You still don't get it, do you?" "What?" "Life. It's not who you are. It's who you wanna be, right?"

There was a girl in my class. Kendra. Half-caste, though you can't say that now. Long dark curly hair, beautiful skin, big brown eyes. Clever, too. Dead clever. Fostered, white family. She didn't fit in, she was better than them. Better than anyone. Picked for the team every time, not that she cared. She didn't give a shit about owt. Fifteenth birthday, she packed up and left, just like that. Kendra. Bet she never, never looks back.

Sound of a teenage girl laughing.

I went into work today. Porters are winking and pointing. Another lot look through the glass doors and laugh. One of them holds up a magazine, opened up and there's Kimberly or Samantha or whoever I am looking back. One of the doctors came on the ward: "I didn't know you with your clothes on". I went out for a fag quick, rang Gary. Voicemail. Tried again. And again. Thought for the first time in years about ringing me mam. And I might have if she weren't still with him, if she hadn't sided with him...

The teenage girl laughs again.

Still, it turns out the lads at work love it. They say "You really are crazy!" They're joking and teasing and pulling my leg, asking me out wi' 'em, all sorts. Course, then Matron calls me in.

"What've you done now?"

"It's a few dirty pictures, that's all."

She shuts the door.

"What the hell are you doing that for."

"The money. I need it, I can't live on this."

"Train up, then. Do exams."

"Me?"

"Why not? I'll back you, I'll support you all the way. You're the best girl I've got. You could be an RN if you put your mind to it".

The teenage girl laughs.

Registered? Yeh, right. I'm not going to college, no way. Cos it's like Gary says, this is me now. It is.

This is Kendra.

Scene Four

November. 3am. JULIE *comes home from a club. She staggers into the flat, drunk.*

JULIE. I was on the box again tonight. Sky Channel nine-o-summat. Garage Girls. We made it months ago at the tyre-and-exhaust place down the road and I tell yer, the mechanics were all up for overtime that night. And we're not just on telly, we're selling all over. We're in business, me and Gary, we're partners. He's got all these machines in his garage. Three films – fifty dollars, plus postage and packaging, he's running 'em off day and night, day and night, day and night... *(calls)* Lulu?

JULIE *takes a small bottle of vodka from her bag.*

We've got a website an' all. It's not strictly legit but so what? We advertise films what aren't certified but like Gary says, you've got to give the customer what he wants. And we don't even need film crews no more. We do a live cam together, that goes down well. I bring blokes back from the club and we secretly film 'em shagging me. I had one last night. Wayne, I think he were called. So? Serves him right, I say. He watches 'em, what's the difference? And if I can make summat an' all, why not, ey? Why not?

JULIE *kicks off her heels.*

Course, for now, all the profits go back in the business. First rule, in't it? You're developing. Growing. Investing, you see? In the future.

JULIE *finds her alarm clock and winds it up.*

Good job we are, an' all, too. This morning, at work, I get in,
do the rounds, as you do. There's a lady, Mrs... Allenby... in
with dementia. Six stone, keeps asking for Mother. I sit with
her, holding her hand. The boss don't like you doing that but
stuff him. Stuff him! Cos that's why we're there and you can't
walk away. You cannot... well, I can't. Never have, never will.
Old and young, I just can't...

I started on Paediatrics. Years ago now. There was one little
girl once. Cystic fibrosis, the awfulest thing you can have. She
was six years old. Gorgeous. Fighting for every breath. I was
her favourite nurse. I did all I could to make her comfortable.
Don't like them crap crisps they sell in the canteen? I'll bring
her Walkers. Read her a story, make her one up when we've
done every book on the ward. She wants to come home with
me and I tell yer, for two penn'orth, I'd bring her. I would.

Sound of the alarm clock ticking.

One night, I'd been working till midnight. Got home and the
ward phoned: "Come back? We'll pay you to sit with her. Don't
wear your uniform, come as you are." I got a cab straight down,
the hospital sorted it, they thought that much of me, see? Her
Mum's there but she said: "Let Julie cuddle me". She was laid
in my arms when she went but... but it weren't peaceful, not
peaceful at all and...

Right. That's enough now. Enough You've had a fantastic
night, fantastic, so don't spoil it and ruin it, don't...don't...

The clock stops ticking.

Cos you bring it all on yourself. You bring it onto yourself,
every time.

JULIE *winds up the clock.*

Matron calls me in. Door shuts. Here we go.

"Julie, I think you know what this is all about."

"Mrs Allenby? All right, I sat with her longer—"

"The staff have been talking for weeks."

"Staff?"

"Julie?"

Turns out one of the porters – the dirty fat one I bet, who's never had a woman – bought a DVD in last night.

Babes in the Wood.

Early hours, the girls put it on the computer. Can't blame 'em, I'd watch it, an' all.

"Just so long as the patients don't, ey?"

"This breaks my heart but I'm left with no choice. Julie, clean out your locker. Hand in your badge."

Gross conduct, she said. Or misconduct, I dunno, I weren't listening. Still, I'm suspended with pay before the hearing, so that's good. "Go out tonight, let your hair down," Gary says. "You have to get up for work no more now. You can earn twice as much on your back."

JULIE *looks at the alarm clock and discards it.*

And he's right. And I did. And down the Palais, I'm a celebrity now. I go out on my own, I don't pay for my drinks. Lads come up all the time and say "Kendra, you are fantastic." There's a gang of 'em come in from Sutton. They love me. Love me. They've just been to Corfu, so they're sun-tanned and gorgeous. Most of 'em. Dead young but who cares? And tonight, one of 'em grabs us. "We've got summat for you." "What?" "Wait and see." I've had a few drinks and I'm dancing; the DJ goes "Kendra's in the house!" This cheer goes up and then the song comes on. Take That. My song.

Sound of a nightclub floods into the flat.

"Clear the dance-floor. Not you, Kendra." The boys bring a table, a chair, a white wine, they know what I like. They sit me down. "What's the hell's going on?" Then out come the Sutton lads, one by one. I have to kiss 'em, even the ugly ones. They make a line and start dancing. They're only undoing their jeans. Girls are screaming and crowding round. Off come the trousers, they're stood in their pants, the girls are shouting: "Go on, get 'em off, get 'em off, get 'em off!" The music's blaring and everyone's screaming and I just can't believe it. For me.

They unbutton their shirts, all in sync. Pull 'em off. They're in t-shirts. T-shirts with me on: legs open and flat on my back. I scream, I can't help it. Then each of 'em whips out a mask of my face. The big screen comes on. Garage Girls. And there's hundreds of people all watching and cheering and laughing and chanting my name. Wanting me, wanting...

Sound of the nightclub dissolves away.

Matron asked why I did it. I said:

"It's a laugh."

"I'll ask you again. Why?"

"It's what men want."

"Not all men."

"You sure? Where's your bloke when you're working? What does your son watch online?"

"I won't rise to that, Julie. I'm asking you why?"

"I like lads. I like sex."

"But this in't sex, not really."

"Well, what else do you call it?"

She went on and on. Asked me how could I live with myself and I ended up saying:

"You cut off, don't you? Like you have to in here, you just get on with the job".

"Don't you dare compare all that with this."

"All right, it's the money. The bills: gas, electricity, food. You know what it's like."

"But I'd never go out doing that."

"Well, you've gorr'an 'usband. What have I got?"

Then I heard myself say:

"And I know there's men out there who aren't into that. Nice men, who love their wives and their daughters how they should. It's just my bad luck I can't..."

She looks at me for a long time. Then she lowers her voice:

"If something happened to you, Julie, you know you can tell me. In confidence. Even if it was years ago. Julie?"

Sound of the nightclub and a crowd chanting 'Kendra'.

It's not Julie, it's...

Sound of a crowd chanting 'Kendra, Kendra, Kendra...'
Not.

Scene Five

April. 3:45am. **JULIE** *puts on an old dressing gown.*

JULIE. This is the life, ey? Working from home, it's the future, is this. Cups of tea on tap, glass of wine if you want one. No more waiting for buses, no more twelve hour shifts. No bosses, no aggro. No laughs with the girls but you can't have it all.

JULIE *cleans up the flat.*

The NHS found against me. That's fine. Gary's expanding. He's bought a three-storey house, Forest Fields. Fitted out the rooms like a fantasy world. There's a wild west one with hay-bales, a girly-pink satin one, a pole-dancing one, a big four-poster bed with a web-cam, a dungeon. Didn't like it down there. Gary gets the girls and men pay to take photos. I'm manageress. Got a laptop but spreadsheets an' that, they aren't me. So he says: "Tell you what? Let's go Dutch." Sends me to Amsterdam. Didn't see no windmills or tulips, no wacky-baccy caffs neither. I'm stuck in a room with no windows, playing with myself and talking to dirty old men online. For nowt.

"Come on, Gary, this in't the deal. 50/50, you said."

"You'll see the money, you'll see the money."

"When? I'm flat broke, I can't pay my rent."

"I've told you, it takes time."

"Time? I've made a hundred-and-thirty-two films. I've been with every Tom, Dick and Harry for what?"

I've had a bottle of wine. He's leaving the flat and I come out with it. I says "I'm finished. You're taking the piss. Find some other slapper, I'm done."

He turns to look at me. "Whatever. Ta'ra."

I throw me glass at the door but he's already gone. There's a bit of a scene when he comes for his webcam. "You've had everything else, you're not having that." I had to call Denzil, he sent him packing. Denzil. He looks out for me. All right, he gets a bit of summat in return but who don't? You get nowt for nowt in this life.

So that's that. I'm down but not out, not yet. Next day, I sign on with an agency. Nursing again. Didn't tell 'em what happened at work, why should I? They're desperate for staff. They put me with a couple of brothers. Both in their nineties, real gents. I wash, I cook, I clean. Sort out their pressure sores, shave 'em, the works. I stay over sometimes, watch Downton. But the agency said it was fifty a night. My wages come and it's eighteen. I can't work for that. I've got bills, I've got debts. It cost forty pounds to have Lulu put down.

Kidney failure. Nowt they could do. And I didn't have enough for the ashes, I...

Sorry, ignore me.

So... so there's the webcam been left in the bedroom. I'm in arrears but I'm not going back, not to him, not to that. "Small ads, a tenner," I think. So I get out the laptop, Google the classifieds. Interesting... Free Personals, Friendship, Connections. 'To blonde lady near supermarket with two white carrier-bags, Monday 18th 12:10pm. We had long look. UR very cute, if single and fancy a drink, text. Man on Bike.'

I hope she saw it. He's a good'un, Man On Bike, you can tell. He wouldn't do all that just for a shag. I even thought about texting myself, you know, pretending I'm her? Could be fate that I read it. Could be... but I look down the page, see a link. Click-click-and-click-again: 'Cathy, beach beauty, available today'. 'Vicky, discreet brunette.' 'Nikki. Back and looking better than ever. Luxury apt.'

Apt means apartment, don't it? And you could call this place an apartment. At a push. It's in town and what else do you need? A few kinky clothes and a phone. But this time, I won't let 'em near me. This time, I'll call the shots. Whips and chains, if that's what they're after. I'll get the ones who want to clean up, call you mistress.

So in goes the ad: 'Veronica. Dominatrix. Her command is your wish'. I thought that up all by myself. The phone starts ringing first day. Time-wasters, mainly. Men who want to talk dirty for free. Or who get out the lift on the wrong bloody floor and knock up your neighbour instead. Trouble is, if they're lost, you can't go out looking, not dressed in thigh boots and a basque. You sit there dolled up but it sets you off thinking 'what if he's not what he says? What if he beats me or stabs me, who'd know?'

So I tip Denzil off, just in case. Said I'd say when they're coming and when they should go. "I thought you'd packed all that up?" "I have, duck. This is different. I'm like Frank Wotsit. I'm doing it my way."

Or I would if I get the chance. One prat rings six times, never shows. Another one calls from a phone box in town. Says he's got a specially made loo seat. Wants me to lie me in the bath and he'll put it on top, take a shit. I hang up. The next one sounds normalish. Darren. Just wants a massage. I've not done one before but it's probably a bit like a bed bath.

I dig out my old uniform. Looks good with the thigh boots, an' all. Take-no-crap make-up. Denzil buzzes. "He's on his way." Finds my door, that's a first. I open up. "In you come, then." But he just stands there staring. I think "He must want the full works." "Get in, now", I goes but I've never been good at being nasty. Then I think: 'Blimey, perhaps he's just reading the meter?' "Darren? 'Tis Darren, in't it"? "And you're Veronica?" "Yeh." "You?" He laughs in my face. "You're joking? You'd have to pay me."

Silence.

I remembered them ads in the back of the mags I was in. Dug 'em out – phoned – here I am. My own boss. Two to six in the afternoon, break for the soaps, then nine till five in the morning, that's when you make your money. And I get all the back-up from the company. They advertise on telly, 0890 40 summat so they're big. They're not a poxy one-man band. They're not him.

Sat'day night. White wine's on offer at Tesco. Three-for-a-tenner, 14 per cent. 'Bout ten o'clock I decide to go out on my own. Why not? But as I walk down, there it is. Arnold bus. Next thing I know, I'm getting off at his house. Stand outside for ages. It's freezing. The devil inside of me knocks. Wife comes to the door, says he's busy. "Does he want a brick through his window", I goes, though it's not like I've got one.

Gary comes to the door. Silky shirt. We sit in the Merc on his drive.

"If I can't pay the phone bill next week, I'm cut off."

"So what do you expect me to do?"

Then I only start crying and saying I miss him. I miss all them laughs at the start. I miss the fun. I miss London. He starts up the car. "Come on, I'll take you home." Chats a bit on the way. All about his holiday. St Lucia or summat. But he drives round the side of the flats where there's no-one around. Parks up then pushes the seat back. Unzips his flies. "I'll give you twenty quid for this", he goes. "Well?"

Didn't take long. He puts the cash in my hand. Looks me straight in the eye. Leans in close like to kiss me. Whispers in my ear: "If you ever come to my house again, I'll cut yer, do you hear me? I'll slash you up so no bloke'll want you."

Denzil found me on the stairwell. Shaking, talking to myself: "Why do you let him? You're fourteen, not four. Why do you? Why, why, why, why, why, why, why?"

He'd finished his shift. Took me up, made me a cup of tea. Sat with me on the sofa. Put his arm around me. Big and muscly from the gym. I could hear his heartbeat. "Shouldn't you be going home to your girlfriend?" "What girlfriend?" Shouldn't you go? "If you want me to? Do yer?"

Nothing went on. We just talked, all night. About Gary, about work, about Matron being like a Mum to me. "Well, if she was, you can sort it", he says. "How?" "Go and see her. Make it right."

And then cos I've got nowt left to lose, I tell him the rest. I tell him… and he believes me. Denzil from Security believes me. He tells me stuff, an' all, stuff what went off, how he's done things in life he in't proud of but how now, he's trying to change. He comes back the next night. The night after that.

"I don't know what you're doing here with me."

"What d'you think? I like you."

"When you know what I am? What I do?"

"Julie, I like you for you."

Won't last. Never does. But he said it: "I like you for you."

And it's not like they're seeing me now. Touching me. I get
10p a minute, that's six quid an hour. Potentially, anyway.
Some nights are slower than others but I've lived on less.
Calls come to Essex, they forward 'em. Premium rate, so the
men, they want to be quick. Trick is to keep 'em chatting.
Clock up twelve minutes and you're top of the tree but I can
beat that. I can make a corpse talk, me. You stick to the rules
though. No animals, no kids, no adult babies, no fancying your
stepdaughter, we get a lot of that...

And summat'll turn up tomorrow.

Sound of the distant Market Square clock striking four.

Still, I suppose this is tomorrow.

Sound of the city at night.

Never stops, does it? You see it all, twelve flights up. The whole
of Nottingham. All them trendy new offices, posh student flats.
Little squares of white light in the sky. You wonder who's up at
this hour? You wonder if they can see me. And you wonder if
maybe he's right? Perhaps you and him can... Perhaps.

*As JULIE looks out of the window, the sound mutates into a
montage of all we've previously heard: nightclubs; girl's laughter;
camera flashes; clicking shutters; porn music and a ticking clock.*

I used to love the small hours on the ward; the peace and
quiet. If the patients woke up, I'd sit with 'em, hold their hand,
talk a bit, listen. Cos if they felt better, just for a minute, then
I did, an' all.

Sound of the telephone ringing.

I like people, see? I like helping 'em. And I'm still helping 'em,
in a way? It's a lonely time, four in the morning.

Ringing.

They only want someone to talk to.

Ringing.

Till summat else comes along.

JULIE *answers the call.*

Hi, this is Julie... What am I wearing? Just a smile.

Fade to black.

Lightning Source UK Ltd.
Milton Keynes UK
UKOW02f1238021214

242517UK00001B/18/P